Crystal Clear

By

James Mounchere

Published by

QUEENS   BROOKLYN   LONDON
ROME   SAN FRANCISCO

Dedicated to
May Sheenan Mounchere

My lovely wee lass playing her guitar.

Love ya baby girl. Xx

INTRODUCTION

By Rose Terranova Cirigliano (editor)

SONG OF SILENCE by James Mounchere

James met Lewis Crystal on Kasia's Poetry Page on FACEBOOK. They enjoyed each other's works and found that they shared the zeitgeist of The Beats, a group of writers from the 1950's. The Beat Generation was a literary movement started by a group of authors whose work explored and influenced American culture and politics in the post-war era. The bulk of their work was published and popularized throughout the 1950s. The Beat writings usually pushed the boundaries of acceptance in the 1950s. The original beat writers were William Burroughs, Allen Ginsberg, and Jack Kerouac. They used the word "beat" to describe their free style of writing and their nontraditional crazy way of life.

James felt he belonged to the group, and Lewis quite agreed.

In this collection we find the work of the matured poet, full of whimsy and unabashed truth about the state of the world and hopelessness of our plight. But the enchanted members of his imagination give us pause, and charm us with their lilts.

James' works are best read out loud, because that's when you feel their music.

--Rose Terranova Cirigliano, editor

THE COLLECTION

miles of ill lit corridors,.

candles burning

,under

st, Francis of Assisi,

and other plaster saints,

seemed to gesture,

in their flames.

pictures on the walls wept blood...

and children, striving to live

the magic of childhood,

without the soft breath

of love.

never missed,

we never knew

it existed.

they took our names,

changed our birthdays,

the mentality of losing an old life,

and starting anew.

i never knew the real me,

until i needed a passport.

and was quite happy to find,

i was five days younger than

i previously thought!

Every day, surrounded,

by perfumed smoke and prayer,

nuns mumbling the angelus

whilst we searched for fairies and elves.

found them,

and gave them names.

and spoke to them as a child

would speak to a father and mother,

in the early mornings,

after an ice cold bath,

for wetting the bed.

as someone once said,...

there were summer shoe days too.

some joy.

some respite from the bamboo,

filey.......the sea the sea

how it listened to me,..!!!!

as a boy,

i used to wait for its voice.

there was no choice,

except to accept its wisdom.

the sea ..the sea..as lonely as me..,

bathed my anger,

when i didn't even know i was angry.

some kids were adopted,

taken away,

brothers and sisters, for years,

ripped from yet another family albeit,

our crazy ragged form of one.

wake up, cold bath, bamboo,

family gone.

we kids used to polish and clean

this place,

every Saturday morning.

the brown lino looked like

a murky glass pond,

candleholders polished,with brasso.

once i remember.

i was scrubbing a flight of stairs, (one of four)

steel bucket, wood and bristly

scrubbing brush.

and a grey cloth .

all of a sudden,

smacked round the mouth,

sister Gabriel,

old bent and evil,

grinning.

there was a chapel in this castle,

sometime in the night,

the nuns would go in there,

for midnight matins,

creepy hymns sung in latin..

floating around .

some new kids with big round eyes,

terrified.

they used to walk around,

with rosary beads hanging from their sides,

like a prison warder's keys.

jingling and jangling,.

no music for me.

clinging to each other

in the half light,

terrified,

because you wet

the bed again. all hope had died.

a place of mad music,

this house full of wax,

where your heart beat the drum,

and jesus, played blues

on the sax.

it goes on and on..

thanks for listening.

Mounchere.

***

And the earth breathed a sigh,

and smiled through the smog and degradation.

And the forests sang a song of hope,

maybe this is the eve of salvation.

And some waters sparkled once more,

because of some common human action.

proving that we can change it all,

without blood, without tears or religion.

There are trees here older than Jesus Christ.

mighty, and so strong in their wisdom.

doing nothing but giving us air to breath,

the foundation of our fragile ecosystem,

they´ve watched mankind committing suicide,

in their mad thirst for gold and destruction.

hoping their intelligence will survive,

long enough to avoid total extinction .,

There are huge holes in the canopy of our lives,

you must have noticed it getting colder.

you can taste the filth in our skies,

the hopelessness on every street corner.

it's time NOW to open up our eyes,

and realise that we are all sisters and brothers,

we all breathe in the same air,

so let's try and dry up some tears from our mother.

let's plant the seeds of the trees

that our great, great grandchildren can sit under,

and breathe in natures freedom songs

one love, one life, one future.

let us learn the difference between want and need,

and build on it here ever after

because when the storm finally comes ..(and it will)

all we have is the strength of each other.

mounchere ...5 may 2020 B.P.(Before Pub)

***

Imagine.....

sitting in a concrete bunker,

with bombs falling around you

like rain.

Not knowing if your house

will still be there,

when it's over.

children crying.

family dying,

everything burning,

A hell, here on earth, a demon birth.

legal murder.

little sustenance, just lots and lots

of unadulterated violence.

after hours, sometimes days,

the all clear would screech its sound,

then ragged forms swathed in smoke,

come like ghosts from underground.

postmen bringing letters from far and wide,

telling mothers and fathers

their sons had died. (blah, blah blah and thanks)

three quarters of the young men

from your street,

splattered under the treads of tanks.

never to bloom again.

years of ash and bloody tales,

of gas and genocide ,

far, far beyond the pale.

and suddenly......

it's over.

the war is over!!!!

stragglers come marching home,

bent and twisted, hero´s every one,

to rubble and charred lives.

their world was gone

forever,

only their bodies had survived.

generations of desperation,

bread and dripping held them together.

robin hood criminals came to the fore,

stealing from the rich,

and selling to the poor.

police where the enemy,

hunger makes its own law.

the virus is a breeze, a cough,

a sniff a wheeze.

politeness reduced to..

would you fuck off please.

masking up is the law,

but not many take it seriously.

social distancing is a joke.

most worry over money, economy.

i hope you will all realise

you are all expendable

energy.

fodder for the factories.

hopefully we will see at last,

how cheaply,

we sell our lives.

a life for a living.?

no fucking dice.

(A. Ramble.)

***

I hear the sea...it's calling to me.

mourning me even,

like a mother wolf..howling

for her young

in the still night

of the forest.

this though.....

this penetrating whisper,

this song of the ancients

beating the shore...

evermore

a lullabye

for the world

and its rage.

her age never destroying

her ways

to beguile.

from her blue gentle loving,

to her flashing

wild eyes.

such thoughts are captured there!!

ocean, ocean, wild gypsy dancer!

and then again,

a slow , seething seducer..

a giver a taker....

an actress a faker,

mischievous , mysterious.

and i am her child.

ALL ABOUT A SEA.

***

I sort of know this poetess...

far as i know,

she lives by the sea,...

she waters her great grandmother's plants,

that have grown over the years,

into l giants.,

i don´t know for sure,..

it's just how my imagination sees her.

she knows the woods,

the names of the trees and their properties,

herbs and spices,

and magical devices,

that can transport me

into a green, childlike, innocent calm,

a place where beliefs and the magic

of life,

are spun with a spider webs yarn.

listens to the mice scampering

in the eves of an evening.

i'm sure of it..

whilst writing

her poems and recollections,

in front of her window,

drinking hot chocolate.

strange i can't imagine,

what sort of music she likes.

admittedly she is a junk shop junkie,

marveling at old lamps

and arm chairs.

jewels left strewn,

in the green lanes of time,

a tassel shawl?

an old fine crafted ring,..

jackdaw lady,

she believes in the shining.

do you fly around the chimney pots at dusk?

sprinkling dream dust.

and words, that...

oh i dunno...but somehow... you can trust.

letters, yes and loneliness,

i dare to imagine, are good friends.

judging by the pictures you paint,

with the nib of your magical pen.

A Poetess.

***

have you ever been really hungry,

and skint,

and someone sends you a picture

of their sunday dinner?

and you sit there staring at,

you know for absolute

certain that

DEFFO

is onion sauce

all of a sudden

its food porn!!! ohhhhhhhhhh wowwww,

just look at the shape of those chips,

yeah!! wayyyyy to gooooo!!

a little more sauce over there

.mmmmmm soft round potatoes,

all soft round and steaming

whist the sweet sweet

carrot,

all slender and neat,

seductively kisses,

a rare piece of roast beef.

ohhhhh and the brussel sprouts,

just pouting

to be devoured,

oh such fun we once had,

in the dinnertime hours.

and there and there!!

my sweet cauliflower budding,

right next to

a great, steaming hot

yorkshire pudding.

it's a disgrace....should´not be allowed.!!!

Whose in charge here?

well then.... er, sorry about that.

i'll just go and get me bread and jam then,

Goodnight.

***

THE BLUE..

I can feel the blue,

the deep blue

it is in me,

it is in you,

a birth,

a death,

SILENCE.

***

just before i slept.

i awoke to its chatter

its whispering pitterpatter.

my first greeting

to our wonderful world,

was a muffled "Oh shit"

don't like this one bit.

i can't find one of my only two

clean socks.

the bastard morning mocks me.

i made some porridge.

yuk..another mistake, tastes like glue,

i'll give it to the birds.

There in my kitchen is a mountain

of washing up.

i don't have a washing machine.

a glass mountain of plates and cups and pots

smirking at my steadily growing

pissed offness.

i had to make my tea in a beer mug.

just the thought of going to work

is making me feel ill.

have a nice day people.

***

she talks when she wants to,

but never says that much,

she thinks a lot about fairies

and little folk and such.

she lives her days

in Colors,

some that i have

tried to share,

as she captures childhood

innocence,

in her magical

musical words.

and she carefully

steps the fields

around her,

feet as bare

as the day

of born

she tip toes

through buttercups,

in the eerie

light of dawn.

she would wash her hair

in morns fresh dew,

and sing ballads

in wee folk tongue

and played the harp

of spider webs,

and gave praise

to the rising sun.

her eyes are green

as infant fern,

hair as black as coal,

her skin has an

aura like glow

that lights up the very soul.

she journeys long,

into the days,

gathering herbs,

for medicine and

for tea.

and glides amongst

the great grandfather trees

a child of roots and leaves.

And birds will land

to be in her near,

bright trust splill´d

from their eyes

and she would laugh

in delight,

as they released,

songs into the skies.

who is this fine lady,

who´s every smile

could stay a breath,?

who´s every touch

is a gift of love

a jewel

in life´s treasure chest.

ONCE UPON A TIME:

***

Early in the morning,

a woodcock driving me crazy,

from first light.

so i'm laying here

sun dapple floating over

the blanket,

waiting for the gold to reach my face,

then i will arise.

The woodcock is forgiven,

and i follow my bare feet into

the day.

A comforting chill

seeps into my being,

the silence saying

a cool good morning,

and me yawning into existence,

stretching through my kitchen window,

tiredness falling from me

like autumn leaves.

Breathe...........!!

The dandy-lions

have multiplied overnight,

and the red rhododendrons

are giving it big licks,

tho the rose is playing shy,

i've seen the buds up close,

and i KNOW..in there waits the rose.

The sun is warming now..

no hint of breeze, or chill,

pleasant,

an insistent

title pops into my head,

"The happy peasant."

A picture of a bearded old man,

sitting drinking tea

by his window,

conversing with dandy-lions.

smiling.

yep...this world

can keep its diamonds,

and its blind

and bloodstained laws,

i would swop the lot for a sunrise,

a piece of toast,

and an open door.

Good morning, me lovelies.

***

When time seeped down the walls
crept through bars of steel,
laughed at the chains
that held me in place,
scarred my soul,
and lined my face.
I dived into the sea of words,
and swam there free
everyday a different world,
a different land,
a fresh stormy sea.
when doors slammed shut
on the summer,on
the years of evenings that
slid away
not one trace of memory,
i was laying on a beach,
miles and miles away.
time in chains,
a remarkable adversary,
drowned in the blood
of its own stupidity.
here, i learned what freedom is,
here i learned
how many worlds inside me live,
here i learned the beauty of the soul,
and walked in gardens,
that we have, all.
and cracked every stone
in the wall.
a bird in a cage singing for a sun

he cannot see,
though in his mind,
he flies the winds of liberty.

***

we
did love,
each other
for a moment.
at least i think so,
a smile a laugh a spark,
a passing of flame
a glow of life
in the dark
of the
day.

***

turning into dark the blue just sank

beneath the treeline,

and i am in the park,

with my back to an old chestnut,

playing my guitar,

watching a single blinking star,

and singing songs

that i've never sung before.

and all at once i saw your face,

it never moved me out of place,

never felt anything,

just another human being

passing by.

i'm so glad it doesn't matter anyway.

i follow some notes into the sky,

through shapes of leaves,

from dark and light

while pinpricks of silver

dot the velvet high.

***

ever rolling, running , strolling,

winding its way,

through flatlands, farm land,

hill and dale.

reflecting sky,

y´know that blazing

azure hue?...

and this is the place

where the green meets the blue.

where the blue meets the green,

silent.... serene.

d

r

i

p

p

ing water.

Only for thirsty souls.

These flowing waters,

in the hearts of us all.

let's dive in,

deep, deep down,

let's roll around

in ecstasy,

neath the grandad trees.

here , yes here,

in this place,

where

the blue,

meets the green.

ancient rocks and stones

stand still,

in the stream,

eon sculptured

curved and rounded

seen it all,

no more astounded,

by the childish man's dreams

stand there watching,...waiting

for the songs of silence

to get louder.

so that we can understand,

things no teacher can reach.

things that in school rooms,

no teacher can teach..

green ...blue, and fresh,

clean souls,

in

natures

beautiful loving

caress.

animals laugh at us,

and our childlike

wonder.

as we breathe in

the pure joy,

of this

bluegreen air,

and the river laughs with them,

as we humans blunder,..

from sunshine to thunder..

never learning

to care.

the fox drinks the water,

out of pure habit,

with the field mice and deer,

and the shy bright eyed

rabbit.

Greenblue River.

***

walking through

dreams,

dancing

with stars,

sculpturing

moments,

out of the

rose vase.

ahhhh long

have i paid

many hours

to the moon,

always

the same answer,

soon, Seamus, soon.

silence is golden,..and patience a boon.

***

James Mounchere

May 30, 2019

My wee garden... Wild and wonderful

most of the time, less is simply more.

lots of birds come here....,

no mowing machines,

plenty of trees,

and a nice place to

sit and drink

a tea.

have a smoke,

and just sit around

and see

what turns up.

view from the kitchen window,

where sometimes

I just

sit and stare,

st this tiny piece

of

earth,

with life

walking everywhere.

the bench

that you can see,

was rescued from certain death,

twas saved from

ending up as firewood,

by beer, a truck,

and stealth,(That was a laugh n narf)

it has been here for years now,

same story with the table,

sitting out their days

in a gleam of sunshine,

just like

old

George,

and Mable.

***

one

morning

we danced

and sang aloud,

we laughed,

in joy

and

love..

***

Good morning

The wind isn´t so cold this morning.

the sun is pretty hot though.

shame it's saturday,

and i've got to build a fence....

would have liked to take my guitar

and sat somewhere for a few hours.

maybe write something that

might help change the world.

you never know.

so...i'm off to work,

have a nice day world,..mask up,

be cool, be kind and collected.

love Seamus.

***

some people might say,

their life...

is in a rut,

and the promises

they get

just don´t ever

cut

it.

Going to work longer

for less pay.

smile and take it ..

it's the modern way.

you want time off?

take a holiday!!

you´ve turned into fuel,

expendable human energy..

and you don´t matter

so long as you are alive,

to work, work, work,

in the queen's bee hive,

with no sympathy or sorrow,

can´t afford to be free,

you´ve turned into fuel,

expendable human energy.

now's the time ,

we've had more than enough,

maybe it's time

for a bit of push and shove,

we´re not asking a lot,

just some human decency,

we are people , we are NOT

expendable human energy.

yes..and it's time NOW

now is the time ripe

for a new tomorrow,

it's time to arise,

from the gutters where they flung us,

and take it upon us,

to take back

our right to a life.!!

Tomorrow is the wealth of our children.

SOME MORE THOUGHTS AT BREAKFAST.

***

And the north wind blows so cold,

but never will it extinguish the fire,

and the years, they grow so old,

and the old bones begin to tire,

of watching the earth

bought and sold,

and sinking further into the mire.

all my life, they´ve been talking peace,

whilst selling guns to each other,

and i hear the voice

of humankind decrease

it's now a whisper

where there should be thunder,

maybe you think this is old hippy speak,

but we can´t do nothing,

unless we do it together.

And the north wind blows your mind,

and your sailing on a plastic ocean,

in a crazy hell where the blind lead blind,

and pounded with useless information,

sheep all walking in line,

bleating their way to destruction,

oblivious of the blood and the grime,

and very little hope of salvation.

and you can safely bet,...you ain't seen nothing yet.

***

oh yes i can well imagine you,

posing in your chair,

playing your dreamers games,

building castles in the air.

and though your smiles were diamonds.

you left in the beggar's care.

the beggar done a runner

and left you standing there.

i see your face slowly vanish,

into the inevitable grin of age,

but you still live in a time bubble

where you keep your yesterdays.

like a box of fading photographs,

that tell the truth in spades

when will you realise

it doesn't matter anyways.

i ve known you since i was a boy,

and recognise the change,

its you and a million other folk,

i know, cos I'm just the same.

it's time just passing by us,

it's just the deal we made

tinseltown is falling down,

now the devil must be paid.

There are paths we could have followed,

had we run along with the pack,

no, we chose the path of wondering.

to see how far it is there and back.

Ahhhh the music , the craziness, the women ,

the whiskey and the wine.

no silver for a future,

and spit into deaths

dull eyes.

And..now we both sit by our firesides

and the lights leave one by one,

we never gave it all up to the factories,

we made memories that shine on and on,

and as we walk back through old memories,

i reckon a good deal was done.

now lone wolves, on lone mountains,

waiting for the howl....

in the setting of the sun.

***

so..i see Boris is recovering well,

sitting up in bed,

after being saved

by the brave

NHS.

the self same people he used and abused,

the same people for whom

he stood and

yahood

when their pay rise was

turned down flat

and refused.

Fortune ,he says, grinning like an alligator,

decided he needed no ventilator.

Thanks to the work of those not in our sight,

those who treat kings and beggars alike,

you gave them no future

still, they fought for your life.

so stop cutting their throats,

with your political knife.

Your chance now o dim one

to try and make some wrongs right,

roll up your sleeves lad,

and join in the fight.

i doubt you´ve got the bottle,

no soldier are you,

a danger for the people,

and a delight for the few.

***

well open up your treasure chest

and see what you can find

maybe there is nothing left,

just some pictures in your mind.

you never were a lady,

and this just added to your shine,

and you spurned school education

sayin' life's school will do just fine.

and you never took advantage,

of the beauty that you wore,

nah never once a fake diamond

a fine jewel to the core,

your children were the songs you wrote,

and you took them out to play,

around burning logs in gardens

till the breaking of the day.

i knew then you had secrets,

that lay buried in your tunes,

something dark and sordid,

that made it hard for you to love,

you built up your protection,

by giving all that you could,

to all those used and abused,

cos i believe you understood.

and many, many years later,

i met you, and a child of your own,

and your soul seemed so much lighter.

and those walls inside you blown,

and it seemed the last piece of the puzzle,

had been finally put in place,

seems the dark mist

that ashamed you,

has finally found a happy face.

love seamus. xx

***

Feels like we´re running...,

faster all the time,

feels like something's

coming,

that's gonna blow,

all of our minds.

are we gonna run, run, run, run run,

for the rest of our lives?

Feels like this lonesome

homeblue orb,

is getting bluer all the time,

control, confusions,

the daily dose of trash,

be under no illusions,

it's all bought and sold

for cash.

Feels like i'm just dancing ,

whilst the loonies play the tune,

feasting on lies , banqueting on lives,

while frantically burying the truth.

nothing is sacred,

even all the Gods use weapons of war,

Feels like we're running fast,

but we don't know what we're running for.

i often wonder what the future looks like,

through the eyes

of our children,

will they be running just the same?

or will they rise up from the ashes,

and be a light,

to rectify our shame.

some thoughts on a rainy afternoon.

***

Open the treasure box me darlin,

see what the fairies have left you.

in exchange for your dreams.

see what the busy elves

have created from moonbeams,

and light.

from sunshine and rain,

no ! don´t laugh,

it's true what i'm saying.

whilst you are sleeping,

upon your soft pillow,

the small folk are painting,

the first green on the willow,

the first blue on the bluebells,

and the buttercups gold,

and a smile on the face

of the grumpy old oak.

and they sprinkle the air,

with a sort of pale misty smoke,

and paint a grand sunrise

do these wee fairy folk.

oh yes you can giggle,...

ahhh but you´ll soon beg your pardon.

when you open the window

and look in the garden.

A Fairytale.

mounchere.

***

Thank

you for

this thought.....

i think i saw you,

staring from a small

window,

in a small white house

on the edge

of a sea.

i think i saw,

one of

the oceans

calm cold greys

dancing

in your eyes,

still, and

deep

watching

the iron

sky....sailing

where souls

of

fisher folk

Fly.

A crooked

door

painted green,

welcoming

a path

of crooked stone,

where bluebells

and

daisys

preen,

and there

a window

either side,

white,

but bleached ,

now,

by time

by winds

and tide

A picture,

to fill

a

smile,

a

Mind.

love seamus.xx **A LITTLE BIT OF MAGIC**

***

I walked in gardens with you,

i never knew existed,

you built great cities from pebbles,

and shards.

your wisdom singing in my ears

like a mountain stream,

as you opened doors

into worlds that lay at my feet.

you brought me Hayden, Correlli,

Beethoven, sailing around ,

old stone church walls.

i saw your eyes close.

and your soul sail away,

lit by coloured strobes

that rode the sun,

through panes of every hue,

that streaked your quiet,

bemused face,

in the contented world

of your solitude.

and i opened every gift

like a child on Christmas mornings.

we had tea in cafes overlooking the rhine,

you speaking of roman castles,

and i basking in the sunshine of it all,

you taught me to take off my shoes,

if i wanted to hear the voice of the trees.

and i will be forever in your debt,

for the portion of time

for making my world rhyme

for a while.

i oft remember the buttercups ,

that ocean of shining gold,

in a field beyond the church yard

where a mare had just given birth,

to a black and white tiny foal.

It was summer then,as i recall.

and when it stood ,we cheered and laughed.

i still have the photograph.

mother and father earth just

for the day.

just looked in to say.

A GOOD MORNING TO A REMARKABLE SOUL.

Mounchere.

***

walking on the shore,

just as the dawn begins to break,

oh how many times before, has

my soul bare and naked,

listened to the songs of the waters

calming melodies.

Aloft the seabirds wheel and glide,

covered now in orange glow,

over bright green rocks fluorescent

in the first kiss of dawn,

greeting the sun with piercing cries

exact wingtips scrape the air.

***

some people might say,
their life...
is in a rut,
and the promises
they get
just don´t ever
cut
it.
Going to work longer
for less pay.
smile and take it ..
it's the modern way.
you want time off?
take an unpaid holiday
you´ve turned into fuel
expendable human energy..
and you don´t matter
so long as you are alive,
to work, work, work,
in the queen bee's hive,
with no sympathy or sorrow,
can´t afford to be free,
you´ve turned into fuel,
expendable human energy.

yes..and it's time NOW

now is the time ripe

for a new tomorrow,

it's time to arise,

from the gutters where they flung us,

and take it upon us,

to take back

our right to a life.!!

Tomorrow is the wealth of our children.

SOME MORE THOUGHTS AT BREAKFAST.

Mornchere.

***

And would my song leave this heart

and seek a place for me,

along olde woods where stags do chase,

amongst gnarled boles of wise old trees.

where every bough yields its magic,

for all those with eyes to see.

would that i warmed my limbs

by dry oaks heartening flame,

with dark pushed back a pace,

and here i would sing my song,

no voice could nay disgrace,

under these diamonds in the heavens,

my roof of sparkling lace.

and here i would build a house,

from hazel,moss, and earth,

and flat rocks from the riverside,

would be my humble hearth.

and i would lay in dead wood for winter,

for wicked can she bide,

and would i be a fox or wolf,

and learn how to provide.

***

The moon is full,

and silver it brings

to everyone that has

the courage for dreams,

watching time fly,,

she just sits in the sky,

kissing clouds passing by

and other nice things.

and as i walk....

i hear my shoes

piercing the silence

of the midnight walk blues.

no need to chase,

i can stay in this place,

forever and a day,

if that´s what i choose.

it takes my heart,

to where i call home,

following secret paths,

known to me alone.

no need to run

no need for haste

time does not exist,

in this ethereal place.

tree´s dressed in silver,

leaves new and tender,

if you have ears you can hear her

giving off sound.

the music of ancients,

the sweet love of patience,

the notes of soft radiance

when the new queen is crowned.

so small you feel

under the stars...

we are nothing ,nothing more,

than a grain of blue sand,

in the deserts of forever

spinning dreams for each other

just makes you wonder at

the banality of man.

WALK AFTER MIDNIGHT.

mounchere.

***

did you feel the sun through the open door,

eyes on fire like a fox.

a grin, or perhaps a sweet shy smile,

flying over chimney tops.

and did you lose a second of breath,

as it struggled to find its way to flight,

that exquisite moment in time

when day finally succumbed to night,

Did you see the hunters moon arise

in a space all on its own,

and did reality softly slide away

in silky waves as the sun went down.

ahhh my sweet i see you blush,

just as sweet as any rose in bloom,

peace be in your very joy,

and love your very tune.

Mounchere.

***

And the pest, grins

and takes its toll,

stealing the last breath of the older,

no mind of color,

or call,

with its scythe slung over its shoulder.

and fear, lives

behind its gruesome masks

and swims in pools

of hollow laughter.

Do we know now

how fragile we are?

do you think this could pull us together?

tomorrow you will

all jump back in your cars,

to continue the drive to disaster.

and the sky will weep again,

with the poison,

you made for your future.

now is the time

for change,

can you stop this shit and call me your brother,?

or is the mind control

so deeply ingrained,

that is the way

and there is no other?

we may not be perfect, but we´re family,

and this beautiful orb is our mother.

ignorance

is riding high,

that is the true cause of division,

also, the blood that

is so pointlessly shed,

in the name of every religion.

it's got to change

, right now

or we´re due for total destruction.

THOUGHTS AT BREAKFAST: Mounchere.

***

yea! ...to build

a small wee cabin,

wild, wild upon a shore,

with windows to the sea,

with an unrestricted view

of sunsets,

and harken the gentle roar...

and a fine grandfather forest

behind me,

harmonizing

with this choir.

And to sit there in the evenings

when the work is done,

and lend an ear

to sweet songs

of earth,

neath the setting

of the sun

and to weave fine dreams,

in fireglow,

that wing forever....

.on and on.

on the shore of nature's hearth...

And..there to sit

and

speak, aloud,

spontaneous naked verse,

that leap and bound

from mind to air,

and muse that,

someone hears them,

somewhere...far

across the universe,

and finds some love

in there.

ONE EVENING IN MAY,

mounchere.

***

And the north wind blows so cold,
but never will it extinguish the fire,
and the years, they grow so old,
and the old bones begin to tire,
of watching the earth
bought and sold,
and sinking further into the mire.
all my life, they´ve been talking peace,
whilst selling guns to each other,
and i hear the voice
of humankind decrease
it's now a whisper
where there should be thunder,
maybe you think this old hippy speak,
but we can´t do nothing,
unless we do it together.
And the north wind blows your mind,
and your sailing on a plastic ocean,
in a crazy hell where the blind lead blind,
and pounded with useless information,
sheep all walking in line,
bleating their way to destruction,
oblivious of the blood and the grime,
and very little hope of salvation.
and you can safely bet,...you ain't seen nothing yet.
***

so what can i do?

what can i say?

it was never my plan,

to feel this way,

never even thought i could

but

if the river is a river,

then i say,

let it flood.

LET IT FLOOD.

****

went into the park,..
two o´clock in the morning,
sitting there in the cosy dark,
wondering what the hell i'm doing.
everything has has gone crazy,
my world somehow turned upside down,
sometimes i feel me so good,
other times i'm feeling like a clown.
your eyes burn like fire.
and your crazy soul does me good,
and i like the feel of your spirit,
flower lady,....you stole into my blood
and sleep hides from me all the time,
now in sitting in park,
early in the morning. trying to slow my mind.
sixteen years we´ve been together now,
me and this big old beech tree.
oh yeah she knows a lot of my secrets.
sometimes as i talk with her you see,
and she just listens in the star-shine
to the ways of this tumbling heart.
just cool your horses Mr. poet man,
and take some light out of the dark.
TAKE SOME LIGHT
Mounchere.
***

missed the daybreak again,

the night was long,

sitting here with my six string lady,

hoping to maybe,

find the chord

that will finish the song

once and for all.

sometimes the stairways

to your mind,

get lost

and are hard to find,

just like the evasive

last chord

of the song,

playing hide and seek

the whole night long.

The night is still, and burning.

shadows cast

by candle flame,

just sitting here stroking

her slender neck,

kissing the frets with tenderness,

i think it just started to rain.

and as i hold this warm body
,she´s
trembling with effort
as she searches every
corner of my soul,
for the elusive note,
to bring this to an end,
the night can be a bastard,
but tonight
she is my friend .

soon old mamma sleep,
will pour sleep into my eyes,
for now she just patiently waits,
she knows there ain't no compromise,
someone, stole the sunrise,
so there's no
dawn,chorus
or goodbyes.

faint light i see now on the horizon,

as the night to daylight shifts,

and somehow ,someway

i begin to realise,

the last chord ,

doesn´t exist.

then the song flys out of the window,

with no thanks

for the hours we shared,be

that as it may,

i´m feeling free now,

so spread your wings

little bird......

see you tomorrow in the real world. xx

SOMEONE STOLE THE SUNRISE

Mounchere.

***

The morning came creeping

over the rooftops....

the sun strained to say hello to

the sky.

sulky clouds

dressed in grey,

unimpressed

by the day.

a cat

flits like a shadow,

in my sight,

one haughty look,

and she

is gone in one

blink

of a green eye.

The garden is wild now,

an army of

Dandy-lions

prowl,

amongst the fern

and

lush wild grass.

the trees

are moving to make

an arch.

an eerie green

almost touching,

invisible

to the eye,

holds my soul for awhile,

aroma of wet moss,

and the sweet smell

of infant growth.

Mrs. Blackbird,

is turning over old leaves,

listening,

busy,

and wary.

kitchen widow Kino.

time for a cup of tea..........have a nice day.!

***

Thinking things into simplicity,

and came to the conclusion,

that nothing matters really.

***

A BREATH OF FRESH AIR.

Sitting within a circle of trees,

on a small hill.

me reading poetry,

she,..painting a butterfly

on a stone,

shortly before sundown,

the sky brimming

with red and blue.

which also bejeweled

her liquid brown eyes,

in one golden moment,

that took my surprise ,

and my words died,

in my throat.

and just for a tiny taste

of time,

i had a glimpse inside

her world.

i called to her

to come and watch the sunset

to see how far it is

from here

to the edges

of the earth.

we breathed in the air,

and shared the last song

of the birds,

as i felt her gentle

rage

somehow or other

we found the same place,

for a butterfly stone,

and an

unfinished page..

mounchere.

***

We had fun didn´t we?

seeing how many faces

and forms we could find,

in the bole of the old grandad tree.

The best one for me,

was the tree within a tree.

you saw grumpy wee elves,

a thousand years old,

playing pipes and holding

lamps,

and love hearts in the

clinging roots.

laughter wasn´t hard to find.

no people, no dogs. no cars,

just us,

happy under an ancient beech,

with evenings flame

touching its bark

and gentle laughter

glid its way,

twixt a purple red dusk,

and dark.

No penny

for your thoughts right now,

but some silver for

your

heart.

DOWN AT THE BEACH;

Mounchere.

***

An oldie from Oct 2017

Amongst my words,

I thought of you,

the infant sun

streaking across my writing table,

warming the paper,

illuminating the tea stains

and the cigarette ends,

that carried me through the night,

tired and worn

and lacking the courage to dream,

I watched the dawn

come creeping in,

seeping through my window,

carving its way through the smoke

into my eyes.

into the empty tunnels of my mind,

into the great halls,

and there melts its music down the walls,

my ashtray overflowing,

like a waterfall of burnt dreams,

never no more, never no more,,

what can I do with this love?

except wrap it in poetry,

and stash it in the cellar

along with all the letters

thine eyes will never read

never no more, never no more.,

***

cranes flying

over

a field

full of

poppies

and

cornflowers

sky blue,

no cotton

cloud

a still in time,

no more

flow the hours,

a deep breath,

and the ghost

is at liberty.

i have no words

for this beauty

i turn my face

towards the sun

not for then

nor for tomorrow

had

this moment

first

begun.

now my back against an old oak,

a hunting buzzard my only muse

shade here....like the soft touch of a lover,

painted in a thousand hues,

a cat comes strolling by,

stops cold as she catches my eye,

any small movement, and she will fly,

for now she just stares and survives.

***

on the stairways in the dismal

blocks of flats,.

where children gather

to inject the dreams

they can´t seem to master

in reality.

are there any dreams in reality?

or did they die in the last pleading breath of empathy?

sympathy turned to savagery,

looked him in the eye,

and cried...

"release the dreams you have tortured and buried in your
burning thirst for death and lies."

and on the walls of the tenement halls,

are sprayed the voices of our souls.

from the pains of isolation,

deep in the tunnels under the roads.

everyday the stories get bigger,

and the danger refuses to hide..

they sell you calm from a bankrupt heart,

when that same heart is petrified.

and lo and behold the angels came,

riding shotgun in the sky..

the sun gleaming on the last tomorrow,

the kids on the stairs don´t really mind.

deep in their hollow they are safe,

from the insane hand of mankind.

A. Ramble.

***

From 2014

Does thy vanity know no depths?

mirror mirror on the wall,

do ye know the truth at all?

behind the eye lives a cunning fox,

the smile as soft as an autumn morning.

holds sharp teeth, that give no warning..

ye lost ye´re soul in the twists and turns

of life's winding ways,.

ye exchanged your castles for fortresses,

in which ye paint ye´re days.

oft times red, and sometimes blue,

ye stand and pose alone

thy tired shadow tries to dance,

steps youth has forgotten..

daylight shows the lines you hide

that drag thine eyes open wide,

but still ye see nothing..

thorn upon the rose.

poor old sheep dressed up as lamb

who knows what sea´s ye sail in sleep,

mirror mirror on the wall,

please grant me one last peep.

i love the words ye use to colour thyself,

even though i know

ye trust them not.

i would ye fade like sundrenched fern,

not as a paper rose in rain,

***

March 2017

A breathing of the wind

I don't know you,

But I can fill you,

I don't see you

but still you are there,

you talk to me

I don't hear a voice,

I walk in dreams

I'm wide awake though

I can't love like that

but you shall live,

And the traces of kindness

Die happiness will give me joy

..... and one day......

will you tell me about your journey

and I tell you mine

***

well open up your treasure chest

and see what you can find

maybe there is nothing left,

just some pictures in your mind.

you never were a lady,

and this just added to your shine,

and you spurned school education

sayin' life's school will do just fine.

and you never took advantage,

of the beauty that you wore,

nah never once a fake diamond

a fine jewel to the core,

your children were the songs you wrote,

and you took them out to play,

around burning logs in gardens

till the breaking of the day.

i knew then you had secrets,

that lay buried in your tunes,

something dark and sordid,

that made it hard for you to love,

you built up your protection,

by giving all that you could,

to all those used and abused,

cos i believe you understood.

and many, many years later,

i met you, and a child of your own,

and your soul seemed so much lighter.

and those walls inside you blown,

and it seemed the last piece of the puzzle,

had been finally put in place,

seems the dark mist

that ashamed you,

has finally found a happy face.

love seamus. xx

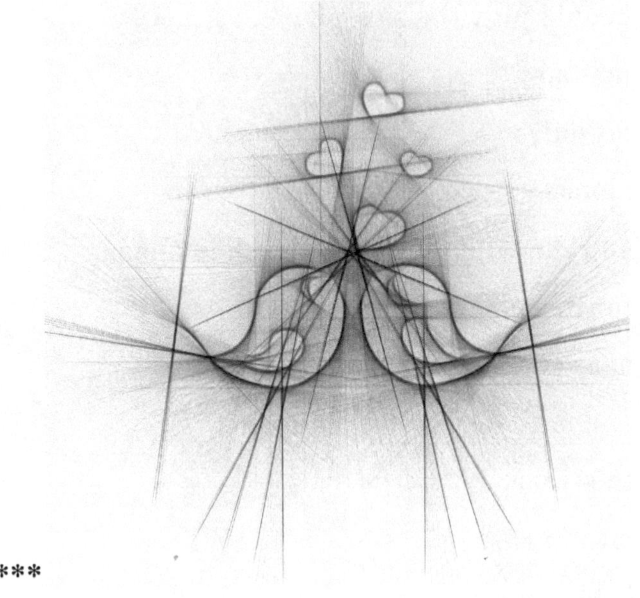

***

well, here we go. .another evening

of another day.

so relaxing,..

i forgot to take my hat off.

is there any other way?

and the light slowly begins to fade,

and nice shadows fill the room,

just waiting now for evensong,

when the birds sing their sundown tune.

its times

like this,

i wish,

i could play the saxophone,

just me,

myself,

alone.

and the windows in the kitchen open,

to the pulsing

beat of spring,

and noticing,for the first time,

this year.

me old rose

is blooming.

now there´s a smiley thing.

sometimes things get out of rhythm,

and things get all confused,

but try not to miss the rain,

cos if you do.....

you

lose.

AN EVENING IN APRIL.

mounchere.

***

put in a circle of trees,

on top of there on a small mountain,

I read poetry,

and they marlen stones

The doom is full of bleeding,

And for fire the sky beautiful,

and no, not just to heaven,

but also in the dien

Smile,

DOWN FOR.

***

cranes flying

over

a field

full of

poppies

and

cornflowers

sky blue,

no cotton

cloud

a still in time,

no more

flow the hours,

a deep breath,

and the ghost

is at liberty.

i have no words

for this beauty

i turn my face

towards the sun

not for then

nor for tomorrow

had

this moment

first

begun.

now my back against an old oak,

a hunting buzzard my only muse

shade here....like the soft touch of a lover,

painted in a thousand hues,

a cat comes strolling by,

stops cold as she catches my eye,

any small movement, and she will fly,

for now she just stares and survives.

***

ein atemzug des windes

ich ken dich nicht,

aber ich kan dich fulen,

ich sehe dich nicht

aber trotzdem du bist du da,

du sprichtst mit mir

ich hore kein stimme,

ich wanden in traumen

bin aber hellwach

so kan ich nicht lieben

aber du solst leben,

und dien frieheit spuren

dien frohlichkeit wird mir freude geben

.....und eines tages......

wirst du mir von deiner reise erzahlen

und ich erzal dir meine

***

TRUE MAGESTREE

(3,200 year old giant mammoth trees.)

In all the years

he stood and watched,

massive changes before him stream,

no words were ever spoken,

no promises where,

made or broken,

`twas just nature living,

her incredible dream.

Then came man chopping,

tearing, slashing,ripping

scars onto her very heart,

never once heeding the warning,

man ...oh stupid man,

´tis but for her, thou art!

Mounchere.

***

seven o´clock in the morning,

no sleep again last night, so i

missed day breaking.

ok call me crazy,

i just like making pictures

out of clouds.

every day the show is different,

just the canvas stays

the same.

and oft i see you in my oceans,

and along winding country lanes.

The breakfast table is never lonely

there is always me, and my ghosts.

watching movies in the sky,

over tea and toast.

Anyway, the day has blossomed

golden, like they do in spring,

another blue skied luvly morning,

some sanity

amongst this crazy thing.

Hey! i nearly forgot to tell you,

there was a robin on my window sill,

sat there just staring through the glass,

as though it wanted to tell me something.

was that you me bonny lass.?

i never once told you i loved you,

just thought you knew it anyway,

i loved you then and i love you still,

there you go,me darlin girl,

i said it for you today.

diamonds and pearls are worthless,

when the piper calls the tune,

all the wealth i've ever owned, was spring,

and now that belongs to you.

see you in the clouds tomorrow,

maybe you can listen to me play,

a song i wrote for you last night,

nothing much.....

just saying "happy birthday" love Seamus.

The duke of Mounchere.

,

***

Give me back my quill and parchment,

a candle to light these newborn words.

let shadows long and nimble be

my timepiece,

the yap of the fox,

the screech of the hawk

my music.

let me lay upon fresh reeds

for my bed,

and a humble heart, and flame

be my love.

let me wake with the dawn,

and sleep in the arms of the moon.

let me know each breath I take,

is a gift from life,

for all life.

let the forest protect me

from cruel winds,

from foul deeds,

and the endless prattle

of man.

Let my mind fly free

And find wisdoms in contemplation.

Let my voice ring true,

When I sing to the silence,

When its whisper.

Has become too loud.

Let me smile in contentment

As I watch my recollections

Frolic in the meadows.

Let the rain teach me songs

That no voice can ever master.

Most of all

Let peace be both

Mother, and father.

***

I'm missing you,..

your dark brooding frowns,

and eerie light.

the purple carpet of your heather,

hugging the earth,

as far as the mountains,

where the lonely eagle gildes.

seagull cries,

over a calm moonlit ocean,

just moments after,

the sun takes her crimson cloak,

and leaves these majestic skies.

until next we see her rise.

over the lonely mountains,

where hawks and kestrels bide.

The smell of woodsmoke comes

lounging on a breeze,

warm glows

of firesides

sprinkling the hillsides,

appear then disappear,

in the boughs of mighty trees.

and huge monoliths

silently watching the way of the stars,

could be anywhere really couldn't it?
But tonight it's in me.

***

The evensong is upon us,
once again,
she soothes the sad earth,
with her soft silver light,
touching
all with her magic,
all within sight,
shy with her wisdom,
full bloom in her flight,
and you just know in your soul,
it's gonna be alright.
Goodnight.sleep tight.

***

I thought i saw some words,

echoing in your eyes,

frightened almost,

timid,

like a bird before it wings

the sky.

and i wonder why,

and i wonder why.

I watched you walk away,

as though i was in sleep,,

an eternity almost

silent,

just the rhythm of

the heartbeat.

big boys don't cry,

big boys don't cry.

yes here we go,

yes, here we go again,

please don´t let me

miss the rain.

Mounchere.

***

me and my angel part **3**.

I am in the woods now. ohhh it smells delicious. All that new green sneaking out filling me with a sense of power, as in energy power.oh I wish I had an elephant I could ride on, and one of those Mongolian hairy jackets.. I hear echoes of "imbecile" coming from my inner angel, which is I must admit, a refreshing change from fucking idiot. I don't take much notice because fear can do that to a spiritual buddy, especially one the lacks knowledge in the basics of survival. Actually she should be pleased, because, even saying it myself, I make quite an impressive hero, even though my cosmic breathing has gone a bit haywire.

I have to accept the fact that even as a dyed in the wool pacifist, I have my lapses, and demanded she slings her hook and finds herself another host.

She just scowled and called me a turd. I googled the word, and found that this word has nothing what-so-ever to do with "imbecile"or "fucking idiot" which gave me grounds to believe that our relationship was improving for a second.

maybe the manual is dry by the time we are home again.

scouring the wild terrain with my eyes all scrunched up like a proper scout,

I spied a bench that the forest department had left for the comfort of pioneers, it was cunningly disguised as a tree. I would have missed it completely if there wasn't a little old lady sitting on it. my spiritual buddy asked me if I wouldn´t mind rubbing some crystals on my forehead and sing an anti-cretin chant. This is new to me, so i refused on the grounds that i needed my concentration for the danger that was before us, an old lady with s yorkshire terrier with a pretty nifty red ribbon tied to its head. And prepared myself to defend my beans and custard creams to the death.

Me and my angel.

Mouchere.

      ***

So.. Here we go. All showered and ready to get out into the woods for a couple of hours. I did make a flask full of tea, but something's wrong with it and it's leaked a pool inside my small rucksack. Ffs. Again my inner angel is hurling insults at me. Ita Amazing how many words you can find for fucking idiot when you really look. My inner angel is really beginning to have a negative affect on my cosmic breathing. But at the same time helping me expand my vocabulary. The package with the peace and harmony section of meditation arrived. But unfortunately it is now swimming in a pool of tea and some other earthy looking substance in the bottom of my rucksack that I can't identify. I am now going to select a practical jacket to wear whilst out walking. Something light. Snot proof, with enough room pocket wise for my Swiss army knife and my collection of fire making materials just in case of emergency. Like if I get lost and have to spend years wondering about the woods. I will also be taking my construction plans for a politically correct survival den, so I need to be wise about my choice of survival attire. My inner angel is pissing herself laughing at the moment, she obviously hasn't any experience in survival tactics. I know it is not politically correct to feel superior to anyone ot anything. But I'm going to give it a blast anyway. I feel like a pioneer on the wild frontier. The thing is in these times is all the people isolating at home bring their dogs to this same woods for waste disposal. (how's that then for a bit of slick vocabulary baby)so all of the fresh dandelions and things of that ilk I had envisioned making a salad from will be most likely covered in dogshit. Bit of a lapse on vocabulary but there you go. I am also thinking about burying some beans and custard creams in the woods in a waterproof container.. Just in case the supermarket is closed tomorrow. I will also take some toilet paper to bribe any lurking zombies that have a penchant for custard creams. My

inner angel says that she has never met such an idiot
in her whole career as a spiritual buddy, and wants a
trial separation. She will have to wait until the
manual is dry. Jeez they never give over nagging.

***

I've had the sniffs for about a week now,

my bathroom mirror speaks to me of doom.

I went through a published list of symptoms,

numbered one to seven.

And I had the first five. o shit.

I didn´t have the courage to read the list any further.

can´t see the point in wasting toilet paper.

Its six-thirty on a fine spring morning

And I'm wandering around in my boxers,

and a t-shirt with tomato soup stains

all down the front,(The latest in quarantine fashion)

smoking the rest of a jolly

I found lurking in the kitchen ashtray.

wondering if I should do something creative

like, build an ark or something.

But Nah..to be honest, my income would just about cover

a very dodgy raft at best.

so I built one in my mind.

A bit like meditation ..y´know?

i got right into it.

even hit meself on me thumb with the hammer

a couple of times.

Then sat and thought about the choice of things

I would take with me.

Only then I realized it wasn´t raining.

oh, I laughed and laughed.!!

so..i built meself the worst sandwich

I have ever made in my life for breakfast,

you know, one of those mad sandwiches where you

just grab anything edible out of the fridge,

and stuff it all between two slices of bread,

whilst absentmindedly wondering if those

little green spots on them can kill you.

well, nothing ventured, nothing gained...

if I die then let this be a warning to you...little green spots

are dangerous.

So what to do with today?

I've not done so bad really considering.

ivé built a raft and packed it with stuff,

and its only quarter past seven.

my inner angel is trying to get me to learn

knitting online.

jeez..the worlds falling apart and i should learn knitting!

yeah right.

my spiritual buddy needs to expand her imagination a wee
bit.

It's like a voice guiding you..or getting on your nerves.

like, I will put on some music...depending on my mood.

and I will hear this little voice say,

do you mind if we listen to a bit of classical this morning?

And you find yourself answering.

No chance.

why not?

Because.

It's kind of like having a discussion with yourself

about your own motives.

my shrink says that's good.

And I agree with her.

But come on...half hours of self discussion about

how many sugars i put in my tea

is a bit over the top.

I read and digested with interest the instruction manual

on meditation.

Performing the rituals etc was great at first.

kind of meeting your inner angel for the first time.

Hey..hows things man?

this is weird, isn't it?

hey ..you wanna piece of cake or something?

you know that lovely first kick of meeting

someone (thing) new. first date stuff.

This manual doesn´t explain how to get rid of it.

it's like trying to escape from Facebook.

my hands are feeling a bit strange too this morning,

I haven't got any disinfectant. so I washed my hands in drain
cleaner. .(.my inner angel says that I'm a fucking idiot)

I'm hoping the package containing the peace and harmony
section of meditation arrives today..

there isn't a virus in the universe that can survive that.

trouble is , it makes your hands look like an

x-ray photograph.

Ahhhhh i've i nice soft light peering through my windows,

i love this early morning light.

my inner angel wants to go out immediately walking

in the woods.

and me in my boxers!!...no consideration some people.

please...will you stfu up.?

Me and My Angel.

MOUNCHERE

---

i dragged my bones from my bed ,
after a loooong night of wakefulness,
normally singing birds lighten my soul,
this morning they just pissed me off.
its one of those mornings when
you try to put both legs in one leg
of your jeans,and stumble about the
bedroom, swearing at the world.
I think i can hear it laughing at me.
bend down to put on my my socks
and smack my head off the wall.
kitchen....one last decent tea bag left,
but it´ll have to do.
one Yorkshire tea bag = four german tea bags,
i'll probably be drowned in teabagist
comments later,but for now i dont give a monkey's.
open the windows wide..
let a bit of the springy air inside,
jayzus, its minus 2 grad...half inch weather.
i love mornings like this.
they make me realise how much of an animal
i still am.
heyyyyy calm down me lad, my inner angel cries.
what do you have to do to get
some peace around here.??
kettles boiling now, went to reach for it,
stubbed my toe on the oven.
i looked my inner angel in the eye,
and thought...one more word out of you mate,
naturally there's no milk for the tea,
now that really pisses me off.

even the birds stopped singing
for a couple of seconds.
maybe the morning newspapers can save my ass,
virus, virus virus virus virus..and virus.
FFS.
And a wee bit o Harry and whatsername.
Is there no escape.
well ...at least there is no chance of the jehovas
loonies banging on the door.
or people collecting money for the blue hair
knitting circle...or similar.
have a nice day.

***

fields running before us,

the part where

death is just an invisible wisp of smoke

amongst our wonderful days of life.

we build castles in the clouds

we build perfect lives in our minds

and doctrines that blow away the smoke of death,

in crazy eternities of joy...of love and of peace.

eternal life eternal love.

In truth we are dust.

we return to the earth the humus ,

we are the trees,

under which our great great great grandchildren

will sit in the shade.

let our seed be strong enough

to prevail .

***

Living alone.

ohhh for years and years now,

silence is a constant companion,

but the choice is mine,

for how long he may sit.

at my hearth.

i spoil his work at times,

when i transfer

thoughts i have gleaned

from its valleys and chasms

into songs and things,

lasting at times,

til the blackbird sings.

sometimes i play memories

on the guitar,

and sing them out loud,

and silence sits there

and grumpily listens

to the fire and ice,

songs for the life of me

i could never

play twice.

sometimes i write them down and call them poems.

silence likes it when we do that.

***

Roll out of my pit,
early morning,
just as the light,
nudges the night,
into wakefulness.
birds chirping their songs
i grope
for the makings for a brew.
same old..same old..
nothing new....
just another day in the life....
fuck there´s no sugar.
i sit and watch the shapes
slowly take
their leave from the dark mass
and become trees once again.
i have this strange feeling
of anticipation,,
like a morning star in my stomach,
faintly glowing awake.
oohhh yess!!
today when i see her,
i'm gonna give her my number,
really this time.
cool as a cucumber.
oh sexy sandy,

the train ticket inspector.
But ...how am i going to do it,?
last time i blew it,
when my courage sank
into my bladder,
and i wordlessly grimaced
a silent greeting,
whilst eating the paper,
i wrote my phone
number on.
must be the uniform.
so....i'm thinking,....
what if she has a boy friend..?
what if he´s a Hell's Angel ?
or a green eyed loony
with no control?
would i be found dead
near the railway track,
with my telephone shoved up my ass?
There´s a moving landscape before my eyes
and the train goes,
clickety-clack.

***

I gave you all my love,
because i am your mother,
and you are my children.
And as i spin in anguish,
blue and alone,
you turned your faces from me
and plundered our home.
i gave you glistening oceans,
strong and full of life.
Forests to love
your breath above
running waters cold
and
all you saw was gold.
I gave you life,
and i weep,
for all you seek is death.
in all around you,
and the blood from each other.
i gave you all my love,
and a beautiful garden
all gone all gone
all sold.
MOTHER EARTH. mounchere.

***

coffee went cold,

but..yeah the sky was

blue and gold,

tasting the first sweet

wisp of spring,

hazel lambs tails,

snowdrops and things.

There´s a green haze

like a mist you cannot see,

the gold of the sun

now, warms my face,

but the haze,

you can only feel.

......it's cool i brought some tea.

****

i saw,

wild white horses

in the sky,

in diamond surf,

and splashing cloud.

wrought

from dawn mist

and part art

of eye,

sculptured in

the realm

of solitude.

iv´e seen your face

in form,

edged in a lace

of blue and gold,

when clouds where abound,

warm and content

in my armchair,

i remember

the taste,

and the sound.

i have seen cotton-wool worlds

pass by my window,

meadows,

hills,

castles of yore,

and i will see them.

forever see them,

until the time comes,

when i see them

no more.

    ***

<u>Solitude</u>

Solitude,
a teacher, a hard master,
a purifier,
a definer, of self,
a mirror of truth,
and alas an enemy of sanity.
A window
through which reality
is seen cleanly
and clearly.
A place to reject.
A place to learn to accept
the darkness,
and build new fresh light.
A place where
to watch the river
of life,
in all its ebbs and flows.
A place to plant trees,
in the desert
of your soul.
A vacuum
to contain
the cleansing howls
oh in this secret glen,
where treasures are found
in the delicate moments
that live in the sound
of silence.

wisdom, with its infinite patience,
smiles, lovingly ,
as she shows you where to look
amongst lifes horrors
for its wonders
and its Colors..

***

The roaring dragons
are chasing Old man time
back into forever,
back into nothingness
our true non existence.
mankind makes merry
and the forests burn,
and the sea´s weep,
wars peep with fire eyes,
we´re running faster all the time.
The peace..the silence,
lost in constant waves of violence,
in greed for the things we think
we need
to be complete.
when our earth has completed
its turn around the sun,
pop corks clap hands everyone,
for the new year's arrival,
personally i celebrate,
another revolution of survival.
how can such a mass of beautiful minds
be so stupid.
Happy new year to thee and thine.

***

you are living your life on the edge now,

walking in mists

none of us know about,

still you have your birds,

that sing for you

in the evenings.

small things like dew on a bloom

you delight in,

the shape of a tree,

the bark of a dog,

a formation of clouds....

you feast on your life.

and glory in its days.

so much courage,

so much wisdom and truth.

you still have the fire

in your eyes.

you have reality multiplied,

and you bathe

in the wonder of it all.

.....and i watch you

a tear waiting to fall.

your mind leapt,from..

one mountain to the next....

remember the day we saw

the foal born?

everything just stopped,...the stones

from the church and the humped back bridge,

where washed away

in the warm tide

of that moment.

now all your moments are so,

it's a dark path,

but you have the light.

each bite of fruit,

adds pleasure to your face,

it is no apple more,

tis a gift from the earth,

a child of the trees,

you know too,

that you are its daughter,..

and as the leaf,

you will fade, back to the mother

of all life.

and you shall be an energy,

for tomorrow.

as you were yesterday.

The Day The Foal was Born.

Mounchere.

***

Thinking of you today.

Thanks for being there.

These last few months have been dark,

then you came along

with your spark.

words and wisdom,

the fires burning warmly now,

tho frost is at the door,

my self is immersed

in a bath full of peace,

that you with your magic restored.

see you soon,

behind the moon. xx

****

naked she stands now,
her fine gown,
chased up the road
by the wind,
graciously deliciously
swaying in time,
thinly bedecked in
a breath of frost
she was
and she whispered
to me
sweet rhyme.

****

A cut glass of mulled wine

cozy up by the fire,

reflecting flame,

and that beautiful mixture

of contentment...and desire

words become birds

coaxed from the air,

and silence becomes a conversation

with no language nor word.

moving shadows on the ceiling,

fire-glow spilling down the walls,

there is nothing....just this evening,

listen to the silence call.

***

O i wish i could cry now,
i wish i could tear
down these walls of sadness
and build tomorrow
new for you,
you left too soon.
and i for one,
am going to
miss you.
its funny , i start to believe
in an afterlife,
like i believe in
sunshine after rain,
only when i think about,
the folk,
that i would ,
really, really, really,
love to see
again.
***

Today,she left us,
and today i am sad,
may your memories
make my morrows
smile.
and my tears,
wash my eyes.
neither of us believed
in long drawn out
sordid goodbyes.
proud to have known you neely. love
James.
        ***

I bathe in warm reflections..

in candlelight,

i see you in flickering flames.

as i will see you

all my life.

wondering back through the fog,

back to the field,

where the foal was born

that day.

and took its

first steps upon our world.

we talked for hours and hours,

your brilliance

your intelligence,

your wisdom

your impish humour,

your loyalty to nature..

we kissed above the rhue

and laughed like children

just let out of school.

i will miss you..
***

Walking all the day,

Around old buildings,

And fine old trees,

Where autumn winds

Love to play.

Thoughts of the past

Fly around like golden leaves

Bringing warmth and utter joy

From laughter and loves

Eons and oceans away.

*****

I knew the wind would take her,

To dance like a leaf

Walking all the day

Around old buildings

And fine old trees

That sway.. And dance

Where Autumn winds

Love to play.

... And hey,

The silver frost in the mornings,

Still virgin under unwarm feet,

Crossing Billy's park,

On the way to church street.

The Crystal cobbles

The ancient houses

All silent, still, sleeping,

Top of my ears tinglingly numb,

And the light is softly seeping into the dark,

In a cloak of red and gold.

***

I saw a beautiful chestnut leaf

sliding horizontally, perfectly

autumnally, and brassy,

in a weak yellow sunned,

blustery, parky afternoon.

it just glided (Glid?)

serenely by,

i stood and watched it

for a small while,

my lady autumns perfume

in my nose,

and a welcome

in my smile.

***

don´t talk to me about the streets
if you´ve never been there,
and tasted its blood,
and felt its fierce love.
sleeping in a doss bag,
under the false warmth of a cast iron lamp,
inhaling dog piss and earth.
uneven paving stones,
begging the baker for yesterday's bread,
a hug from the local bag lady,
laying with your love of this night,
under a tree,
and knowing ...this is how
it was meant to be.
spontaneous, free and gracious.
still, they sit around their tables
spinning their fairytales
and fables,
still, there are knives in the alleys
for to feed their anxious young.
you think slavery is over?
naaaah my friend it's just begun.
the working class can kiss my ass,
I've got the bosses job at last.
perhaps a smidgen from this,
we all may learn,
don´t sit talking shit
and watch the forests burn.
are you tough enough to love.

****

sitting drinking tea

outside, on a cobbled street,

where i used to love to get drunk

and sit and play

my ragged music

to anyone or anything,

that had the courage

to stop and listen.

bleating my heart out,

for two church towers,

and a moon,

just vomiting words,

plucked from the air,

bells booming along with the tunes.

drunkenness and yes,, obnoxiousness,

and wacky baccy fumes.

worth a small wee chuckle

in life's scriptorium.

PS. i was lying about drinking tea,

i was actually drinking a cold bottle of beer in the

sunshine.

***

DANGEROUSLY
GOOD IDEAS

moon painted mist,

rising like smoke,

from sleeping meadows,

shadows from silent tree´s

move and dance,

like voiceless sea´s.

as far as the eye can wonder.

****

oh where oh where has flown that lass!!
gone like alice through the looking
glass.
sometimes i see her,
not for hours and hours,
as she creeps through the spring grass,
the bracken and flowers.
she said she see´s frogs with hats on,
jackets with shiny brass buttons,
bowing like gentlemen as the dragonfly's bye.
she says she knows small folk,
that make rings of snowdrops,
that appear in the mornings.
she does´nt know their names
so as goes the song...,
when that power is lost,
all becomes real, then
the magic is gone.
oh where oh where has flown that lass,
gone like Alice through the looking glass.

****

mayhap future contact will be by letter.

sail boats and mules, and smugglers silent boots. exchanging

sacks at midnight, ´pon the lonely quays.

****

James Returns

i'm sick of being lonely,....,

but scared of losing my aloneness.

the only place, the living womb.

where i have no fear

of my own madness

who could stand to share a life

with a man on with a quest,

to plumb the depths of sadness.

a world where shared conversations

turn into poems and prose...,

where love is as fragile,

as the blood of the rose.

in a world where things are too real,

where music is for your ears alone,

where your guitar is the heart for secrets,

in the times when the bleeding is done.

no talking on long treks through the woods,

listening to the songs of the streams,

hoping to glimpse a diamond eyed fox,

or a deer as it stands there and dreams.

i love the still, ..i love the silence,

the calm hand of nature,

and the awe in its violence.

i love the rock n roll of storms,

and the lash of the rain

,and seabirds in flight,....,

the long whistle,

of a train ,

in the still

of

the

night

i could never love you,

like i love

a full moon over the sea.

or like the hand that paints magic hours,

in the dawns that speak to me.

i will die old and alone,

on a pillow of words,

im husband to nothing....

my wife is the earth.

****

Time left me,

the days melted into nights,

and the nights stole my sleep,

my mind in a dark seedy place,

where sometimes thoughts of death

told me stories of peace.

tempting me to still my thoughts,

tempting me to still my breath.

to walk the road of sunshine and joy.

I beat them all aside with my guitar,

random chords, repelling attacks,

at the golden gates of sanity

swinging the bloodless axe.

some days forests destroyed the walls,

sometimes the windsong took my attention,

away from heavy blocks of sorrow,

and broke the chain of pain.

smoke soothed the mind wounds.

but left me empty,

left words slipping down the glass,

that separated me and reality.

snowstorms of memories and laughter,

things said, that didn't mean much then,

suddenly became my friends.

until they too began to hurt.

anything and everything you do

to turn back the clock is futile.

time mocks your confusion.

my brother died..i never cried,

I just didn't, and still don't know how,

but visions, words, food , smells, and music

weep for me.

and I gather the corpses of moments.

and build bridges to sanity.

I hit the booze again, but not with any vengeance.

just now and then,

when the nights demons

where too strong.

im nearly home agan now,

the windows need cleaning, but it's okay.

just thought I would share with you

the reason i've been away.

love james.

*****

Rain clouds,
they come
and they go,.
in between,
it rains.
It's just
a part
of the show.
From here,
where i'm standing,
I can see
the edge of dark,
I can see
illuminated rain,
falling
through sunlight,
like a shower
of golden sparks.
Beyond,
is blue,
and freshly
washed ,
the trees
seem greener,
blooms
bejeweled
dripping
drops
of
sun,
reflecting....

like memories,
in fields,
where once
i used
to run.

****

when evening falls,
when silence
drifts like mist,
and coats the furniture
like dust,
when the sun
slants over the rooftops,
and bathes my reading chair,
is the time
when words creep from the walls,
the time my mind begins to paint,
sometimes in colours
I don't recognise,
they are the brightest
of them all,
some pictures in painted words
escape
and fly around the room
like nymphs,
always just out of reach
but always warm and friendly.
today I wrote a mighty mountain,
with water falling and tumbling
from its height.
into a blue lagoon
that exploded into
white.
i've never seen this mountain before,
I made it out of words,..
and now there it stands,
silent in my living room,

amongst the dust motes
Dance.

*****

This morning on the desolate streets of schwelm,
only me and the birds.
breathing in the days new air,
finding treasure in the silence.
dew sparkling on the grass,
like someone had sprinkled diamonds
in the night.
an infant sun climbs the trees,
orange and yellow, the intricate bark
their crowns softly burning,
in the still of the waking day.
The tower falcons are back,
they are building nests,
in the eaves of an old building
across the way.
slicing through the air ,
a symphony of grace and speed.
slowly the town stretches and yawns,
cars and bikes start to appear,
the rattle of window blinds being raised,
and there is the faintest smell
of coffee, mixed with
that early morning greeny smell.
delicious.
ah well, time for breakfast,
put the kettle on ,
and find my old red mug.

****

meant to be life...
like wolf, or fox,
shadows and shades,
no ticking of clocks.
no gun tearing
the curtain
of woodlands
green calm
here hunger is the hunter,
no bullets
or napalm.
Here creatures
give life.
so the earth
may live
never a call for vengeance,
it's given
to forgive.
meant to be wild
but loving,
no threat
to the breathing
soil.
I am ashamed,
as a human,
that we,...

as the dream builders,...,
this beautiful
dream.
did
spoil.
no beliefs
to die for,
no flags
in the wind,
no mad goals
to try for,
no blind leading blind,
it's time for
real action,
no time
left to pause,
there is
only our planet,
and natures grand
common cause.

For may sheenan, with love. Dad.

****

where are you gonna run to boy,
where are you gonna run,?
when all the dust is settled down,
and all the brexit shit is done.
sorry sir, you can't live here,
you ain't in the union no more,
i know you've been here for twenty four years,
pack your tackle and there's the door.
i've been a lot of things in my life,
but never an illegal alien before.
hardcore.
so..what is gonna happen now mrs may?
oh Theresa what the fuck shall i do?
i suppose i could buy me a tent,
and head for timbuktu.
or is that in the fuckin EU?
so... will it be armed police at dawn?
and dragged from dear old schwelm?
armoured cars and tanks and guns ,
with merkle at the helm.
i've been in violent situations,
lived cheek by jowl with war...
i've been a lot of things in my life ,
but never an illegal alien before.
Hardcore.

****

sitting here in the still night,
a faint reflection in the window pane,
i play with this ghost,
with the flame of the candle,
the shadows , and fire,
show me many a different face.
its silent,
except for the tick ticking,
of my old oaken clock,
and the odd drop of water,
its pregnancy over,
squeezes out of the ,
kitchen sink tap.
i watch myself smoking,
the red tip,
reflecting on us both,
there are strange creaks
and moans,
cooling pipes,
cooling in the night.
the last train to somewhere,
passes by.
its rattle disappearing,
like an echo,
in a cave.
sometimes the silence
can get quite noisy.
and the words,
they don't come easy.

*****

Opening doors to other worlds,
where colour flows in endless swirls,
where you can dodge
in between raindrops
if you want....
And all is full of new trains
of thought,bringing
beautiful pictures
of things untaught.
And..you think your mind has blown
away, in the warm winds,
that in this very moment
steal your very heart.
There in the silence,
music is heard,
dressed to impress
the waiting words,
sitting on the sofa,
in the living room
of your mind.
no finer way to speak
with hours,
that fall so gently,
like April showers,
with a happy smile, because you THINK,
you have found a way
to save
the world.

****

some call it heartbreak,
to others, it's just a pain.....
oh if i ever get out of this place alive,
i´ll ever more pray for rain.
sunsets in the cities,
bring me to my knees,
she´s gone she´s gone, im dying,
someone help me pleeeeeze.
every song on the radio,
is aimed directly at me,
o if i ever get out of this place alive
i´ll never more watch tv.
even the smell of frying mushrooms
sends me into a deep despair,
and if i happen to smell apple soap,
then i'm climbing the f.....ckin stairs.
There's some ways people eat spaghetti,
that is ..er , kinda ,unique.?
her way was pure orchestra,
oh just to watch her was such a treat.
the way she sort of became one with her fork,
was knockin on the sublime,
if i ever get out of this place alive,
I'll ever more pray for heinz.!
i'm frantically seeking and end to this story,

****

i wish i could
really show you
who i really am,
i wish i could sit
and watch you,
really understand,
i know, that
im supposed,
to be
immune
from
being alone,
i tell you
some-days,
i am a child,
and i can't find
my way home.

I bought galaxies
with my sorrow,
and hung
stars
in an impossible
sky.
then i hid behind
the moon,
when

my world
needed
to cry.
but
it's
a hard
old place
we live in,
and somehow
must survive.
so please forgive me,
if im not
everything,
you see
behind
my eyes.
everything
thats blue
and nice
doesn´t always
live
in
Paradise.

***

i once met a storyteller,

an old feller,.....

lived up on a hill,

together with a blustering wind,,

perhaps he lives there still.!

dressed in a threadbare suit,

and a fine mane of silver hair,that

framed eyes as blue as never seen,

that saw things in the air

.

he told us of mighty battles,

twixt,the realms of joy and woe,

of goblins and elves, and magic swords,

of mountains of fairy gold.

He told us of the secret lives of trees,

and gave us ears to learn their talk,

and assured us that on certain full

lunar nights,

The little folk still walk.

he told us of fairy boats

that could sail from star to star,

he told us our planet was so small,

you could fit it in jar,!

he told us of middle earthly pirates,

that tried to steal the sun,

the armies of the elves repelled them,

though the pirates nearly won.

he told us of beautiful cities,

built beneath the mount of mourne,

and the hope that fell upon the land,

when the fairy king was born.

and then...and then....

we had to go home for tea.

...on the way home

down the lane,

all of us did agree,

the Stories were all bollocks...

but a fine old feller was he.

*****

You empty the pockets of your heart,
when love decides to depart,
maybe there's still a few loose coins
to get you home.
Maybe some fish and chips along the way.
You can eat them on that Victorian bench,
around where the sparrows play.
And chip by chip you toss them way,
just to see the cheeky sparrows
move like arrows,
with that glint of pure joy
in their black beady eyes.
dive on them and fly away
And i sit there developing ,
an important philosophy
about birds and chips.
Departed love?
Heartbreak?
Nah.
It just lost its wings,
walking through wool shops,
and having to give up lamb chops.

i once met a mate of mine,
who used to be the captain of the rugby team.
Ahh yonks ago.

He was dressed in a lovely
turquoise gown..
i thought it was his mother at first ,
here was a gay festival in town.
Of course i started laughing,
it wasn't really me..
Just my heart it seems.
He was the terror of the rugby field,
back then..the. Ironsides
of our rugby team.
Not cos he is gay or anything,
it was just the two visions
i found amusing. Obviously my new love departed
.. Before i had time to explain...
Goodo..
Lamb chops for tea
The sparrows ate my fish and chips.
Suddenly,
i felt this enormous desire
to have a wee,
standing up,
behind a tree.
The rebel unleashed,
i did just that! Only the sparrows
shared my triumph.!!.
****

you sailed away in a boat,
that i had cobbled together ,
from our dreams,
our dreams where sturdy and strong,
nailed together
with laughter and song.
end of the eighties it was,
and grand time for love.
we painted our house,
all yellow and red..
painted rainbows smiling above
our bed.
the days i watched your
utter life..
bouncing along in the sunshine.
i will never ever forget.

you sailed away in a steel ship,

bound for australia.

the doc said the climate there,

would be good for your illness,

multiple sclerosis,

i would have loved to leap

on board,

Impossible..cos i've got,

a criminal record.

these days my izzy

you live in every swell of the sea.

and this particular ocean,

still lives in me.

maybe somewhere deep in me,

i'm on the shore,

waiting for,
your
return.
i've always been an atheist,
just relied
on lucky seven.
and when you died,
was the only time ,
i wished
there
was a
heaven
i could believe in.
well, it's your birthday today,
and the sea
is still empty,
no ships on the horizon.
but my silly
old heart, still waits
on the shore.
Happy Birthday my love.
for today,
and for
ever more.
love. J.
******

Have you ever met someone...

that makes you scared ,

to look into

their eyes?

not a frightening sort

of scared.

kinda the scaredness,

you would

feel,

if you were

standing

at the gates,

to some

unknown

paradise.

have you ever

read

someone's

writings,

and

really

strained

to hear their voice?

in the silence

of your room

at night,

and secretly

rejoice.?

have you ever improvised

on a sad guitar,

and

sang from your heart,

to a face.?

and the saddest part

of it is

knowing,

it's all

useless

anyway.

Nah, i get scared looking

into those eyes.

****

Blue smoke and mirrors,
with its poetry
of colors,
flowing,
dawn
into
darkness,
a red and gold
river.
in the wee
small hours,
of
blue, smoke and mirrors.
,
fire steals
over the carpet,
over tables,
and chairs
silence,...
touches
the lips
of the morning,
in breathtaking verse,
awakening old feelings,
soul
deliciously shivers,

in the wee small hours,
of blue, smoke and mirrors.

classical radio,
soft,...and low,...
as the oceans ....
soothing,
hushed,
like newborn emotions.
The orchestra swells,
a violin weeps
the candle flame flickers,
as I yield to spells,
blue, smoke, and mirrors.

out through my window,
I see a faint
curling mist,
the breath of an angel
a soft tender kiss......
the world is awaking,
the nerve of life quivers,
thoughts of you
burn,
in the heart, and
the quiet,

of blue, smoke and mirrors.
blue..and
Corelli,
the nights
dream givers,
in this rainbow
lit room,
full of,
blue smoke
and
mirrors.
as I kiss your
sweet memory,
sleep pours
its tired wine
in my eyes,
and I breathe it in deeply,
and begin to realize
it was all smoke and mirrors,
true love

in disguise.

*****

memory lane

memories,
those dusty old tomes,.spines
titled and printed in gold,
the incidents that have spanned
your time,
waiting on the bookshelves
in the library of your mind.

Old faces, crazy places,
the fine old streets of when
you were young.
moments when the rain came down,
other moments
full of laughter and fun.
i like to wander through
some of the yellowing old
pages,
every now and then,
meeting old loves, old mates,
and bruvs.
hey how're you doing?
nice to see you again.
saturdays, was market days,
the smell of fresh caught fish

from the unloading trawlers,
down there on the quays.
the marketplace, a cobbled old square,
in front of the ancient
old stones of trinity church.
the grand faded stalls,
canvases striped red and green,
would add a dash of colour,
to this stoney old scene,
there where cups and plates,
sold and wrapped in brown paper,
up on a soap box,
the stall holder would caper.
juggling with tea pots
and milk jugs,
pepper pots and tea mugs,
he would just stand there.
juggling, and entertaining
with his hilarious banter,
i'll tell you what i'll do...
i'll throw in a salt cellar, too.
three bob, ladies,
can't say fairer than that,
any cheaper and it's
the shirt off me back,!!
pure gold.

eating fresh out of the fryer,
piping hot in pouring rain,
mingling with those people,
some i'll never see again,
except in some of the dusty
old tomes,
on the bookshelf,
back in lifes,
old dusty lanes.
there a narrow cobbled street,
in truth,
called the land of green ginger.
apparently they used to store,
raw ginger there.
i swear,
walking down this street,
is like walking back in time.
the buildings still wear top hats,
and tails.
and it has this air,
of sooty, coal and grime..
rag and bone men with
horse pulled carts,
ringing handbells on a winter morn,
and his call echoing through the streets..
RAAAAAAGBONE; RAAAAAAGBONE:

he would sing,
dressed in a scruffy old overcoat
tied with string.
a greasy old flat cap,
and cig hanging
off his lip.
mrs pages sweet shop.
on the corner of ash grove,
huge jars of sweets lined the walls,
mr page a pipe smoking man,
always dressed in brown overalls.
there was liquorice, bullseyes, penny dainties
all served up in white cone shaped
paper bags.
aladdin's cave, when i was a lad.
ahhhhh there´s thousands
of books more.
lost loves, found loves,
castles, tipis, journeys,
stuff of that kind.
all sitting of the bookshelves
of my mind.
so that's it..time to take a breath,
i hope i haven't
bored you all to death.!
***

Bar room, bistros,

round and round the carousel goes,

bright colored eyes

bright colored clothes.

have you seen the beggars in the shadows.
lonely people drowning in glasses,
waving drunken dreams at the horses,
running steadily on their different courses
everyone.
ahhhh let me off i wanna be sick,
the walls are too thin, the beer too thick,
feel like i'm the brunt of some cruel trick..,
if im gonna die here ..lord let it be quick.
bartender dreaming of his summer crowds,
says your hairs to long,
your strides too loud,
maybe i'm a little crazy , but i'm still proud,
i wanna be far far away from this
maddening crowd.
dark skinned woman with a begging bowl,
got no money,
but a lot of soul,
singing in the street,
old gospel songs,
swing low sweet chariot,
i will be strong.
and she sings from her guts,
oh so much bluer than blue,
to the dead eyes folk, just passing through,
she's got a shine to her eyes,

and that passion in her throat,
but she´s got no shoes,
or overcoat.
there..the poor old man, sitting with his dog,
been living rough,
for god knows how long,
gentle as a lamb,
and soft with his words,
he sits and shares a piece of bread,
with the sparrow birds.....
and the rain keeps falling down.
and the rain keeps falling down.
ahhhh let me off, i can't take no more,
why is it that love,
lives best in the poor,
maybe this light shines brighter
in the dark,
under cheap leaking plastic,
under trees in the park.
i've seen ragged children,
looking puppy eyed into a baker's window,
telling each other what they would buy
only if.....
ignored by the folk that gather there,
ignored by a world,
that doesn't really care.

soldiers coming home from war,
penniless, homeless,
no idea what they were fighting for,
begging in the streets of freedom,
they swore,
to defend.
no bucks here bro..
this is the end....
and a draft dodger comes to be president.???
ahhh let me off i wanna go home,
where-ever that is,
i don´t really know,
just somewhere away
from this horrorshow.
everyone seems
to live on their own planet,
behind the battlements of their lives,
knowing no difference between,
want and need,
no knowledge of what's going on outside.
Blessed be the poor,
for they shall inherit,
the kingdom of love....
you cannot know hunger
if you´ve never been hungry,
    *****

<u>**The wolf...and the heart.**</u>
I am this wolf,
that went to sleep
in its
winter den,
so tired of
the anguish of death,
so weary of the pains of life i
crawled in amongst
the crackling dry twigs
and branches,
and the earth
that smelt of dry moss.
and dreamed
i was me.
human that spoke to me,
through the curtains
of forgotten mornings.
through the cold cold lips
of sanities cruel walls.
saying sleep now, rest,
and dream,
sleep now,..
the time of the lone wolf
is over,
your dream will

take your soul, and wash it clean,
and in the depths
of this winter nothingness,
you will grow,
and become yourself again,
you will be a child,
with the wisdom of an
old wolf.
every mouthful of food
a blessing.
the feelings and thoughts
of others
respecting.
there will be dangers,
when discipline
will win against the
wisdom of the wolf,
but do not falter, for they are
lessons in themselves.

summer came,....,
the sky pierced my dream,
i hungered for life...
and thirsted in my quest, to be
a good man.
slowly,

after many tries
i made it out
of the
door,
trees in leaf, the singing of birds,
the warmth of the sunshine,
took the edge from the
fear.
walking sandalfooted over the grass,
and knowing where i come from,
is under my feet.
anywhere i choose
to walk.

enjoying my wolf dream,
like a child on Christmas day,
don't know what to eat first..
is the wolf now dreaming he is me?
i got drunk,
and loud,
and pitifully reckless,
respect,
held its head in shame.
still does.
As morning came ,
creeping , seeping,

into my alcohol befuddled brain,
and realized that,
discipline
had turned its back
on
the wisdom,
of the wolf ...yet again.

now i'm licking my my paws,
whining like a whipped dog,
but as recently said,
danger lurks,
even in the brightest of joy
and you see the ashes,
and valour of your dream
destroyed...
you must make stone
from the ash,
and from these stones,
build your home
afresh..
and
stronger.
James mounchere. LOVE AND PEACE;

******

Feels like we´re running...,

faster all the time,

feels like somethings

coming,

that's gonna blow,

all of our minds.

are we gonna run, run, run, run run,

for the rest of our lives?

Feels like the this lonesome

homeblue orb,

is getting bluer all the time,

control, confusions,

the daily dose of trash,

be under no illusions,

it's all bought and sold

for cash.

Feels like i'm just dancing ,

whilst the loonies play the tune,

feasting on lies , banqueting on lives,

while frantically burying the truth.

nothing is sacred,

even all the Gods use weapons of war,

Feels like we´re running fast,

but we dont' know what we´re running for.

i often wonder what the future looks like,

through the eyes

of our children,

will they be running just the same?

or will they rise up from the ashes,

and be a light,

to rectify our shame.

some thoughts on a rainy afternoon.
*****

Blue,..just sometimes,

brings me

a face,

comes out of nowhere,

like net curtains,

a fine breeze

has displaced.

and then it just leaves,

blue does that to me

....just sometimes, again.

Another Nice Blue.

.****

what a fuckin way to spend
your fuckin time
in a fuckin room,
that isnt fuckin mine,
with a fuckin steel door,
that's locked by swine..
it's fuckin disgustin,
it's fuckin unkind.
all the fuckin kids needin fuckin shoes,
fuckin rentmen bleating
begging for their dues..
every day the fuckin same.
never no good news.
it's not the fuckin life you´d pick
if you could fuckin choose.
Fucking Hell.
Mounchere..

****

the night,...
is an old woman,
sitting in her arm chair ,
knitting, and watching...
as i write.
the tick tocking of her breath,
is no mark of time
as i plunge into its depths...
my words, my friends, my lovers,
my secret treasure chest,

all the forests, trees and seas,
these jewels can unravel,
all there , in my armchair,
,mostimes....
riding a
train of
thought,
is the
way that
i travel.

magic,spells of my own creation,
the joy and tears,
of these children,
playing in the garden

of imagination,
i have built castles,
in landscapes .and woodlands in bloom,

towers of stone
of all sizes and shapes.
mountains, and waterfalls.
all here..
in this room.

the old. lady ,... she knits spells you know.
she has the chill of
the fairy hours,
and the warmth of
a
winter fire´s
glow.
and in all of all she takes a part,
in all that speaks softly,
in all that
speaks harsh.
sometimes she just talks.
and tells
you things.
Old Lady Night.
Mounchere.
****

Red roses growing on a
whitewashed
wall.
Looking well.
i remember when they were Babies,
all those seasons ago.
skinny wee stalky things,
fixed to a frame.
stalks as thick as your finger now,
i saw them as i was passing,
a took a secret smile,
out of my secret bag of smiles,
and smiled!
sun was shining, belly was full,
then popped out me full grown roses
just to say how do....well y´know....
it brings a sort of nice little
jolt of contentment with it,
put in the lunch box,
save it for later.
something to keep my apple
company.

****

you are living your life on the edge now,
walking in mists
none of us know about,
still you have your birds,
that sing for you
in the evenings.
small things like dew on a bloom
you delight in,
the shape of a tree,
the bark of a dog,
a formation of clouds....
you feast on your life.
and glory in its days.
so much courage,
so much wisdom and truth.
you still have the fire
in your eyes.
you have reality multiplied,
and you bathe
in the wonder of it all.
.....and i watch you
a tear waiting to fall.
your mind leapt,from..
one mountain to the next....
remember the day we saw
the foal born?
everything just stopped,...the stones
from the church and the humped back bridge,
where washed away
in the warm tide
of that moment.

now all your moments are so,
it's a dark path,
but you have the light.
each bite of fruit,
adds pleasure to your face,
it is no apple more,
tis a gift from the earth,
a child of the trees,
you know too,
that you are its daughter,..
and as the leaf,
you will fade, back to the mother
of all life.
and you shall be an energy,
for tomorrow.
as you were yesterday.

The Day The Foal was Born.

Mounchere.

*****

she turned off her smile,.....
just for a moment,
and it rode out of the room,
on a sunbeam.
leaving the space,
leaving a face....
full of deep etched lines,
and cold eyes.
surrounded by a summer sky.
she saw that i saw......
deep, deep into the hollow
brimmed with fleeting shadows,
hanging from the gallows.
of her soul.
uncertain the smile
flickered on again
careful, like a cat.
.scared somehow.
confused, it sat there,
on lips that spoke no word,
but sang of sorrow.
and i played guitar,
and sang
the
refrain,
her eyes cleared....her voice
was born,
and she washed,
her soul
in the rain.
i'm gonna write you a mountain,

i'm gonna write you fields of joy,
try and plant a forest in your eyes.
as a gift forever,
from the heart of a lonely boy.

***

sittin here,
in my faded old chair,.
my guitar
warmin' my old knees.
played a couple of chords
for the evenin' sun,
and the silence just turned
and grinned at me.
the vibrations kinda travelled
through my heart,
and said hello to my soul
and softly kissed my hungry mind,
just because it could.
and i sang a love song
just for you
while the sky started
drippin' blood.
in the background crows
where singin the blues,
and the old clock was tickin its time,
the red and white roses
i stole from the park,
are sittin noddin' in rhyme .
did i tell you today that i love you?
or did we do that yesterday,?
you asked me,
"will i love you tomorrow"
i said"it doesn´t matter anyway."
tomorrow is still blind and deaf,
and doesn't have much to say.

but hey hey hey , it's a beautiful day.

The refrain is the rain,

beating on my window pane.

Boom!

! the thunder kicks in again,

this ones for you

only for you,

a whole skyful of love,

f l e x i b l e

but true.

i could lie to you in "D"

and say , nah, i don't feel a thing,

the mice in the hall know the truth,

and i know for a fact they won't sing.

they have the instincts,

they have the sight,

but hey , can you lie,

just one more time

for me tonight.

JUST ONE MORE TIME TONIGHT;
Mounchere.

***

pushing the barriers,pushing the barriers,

stakes are rising, ever rising...

new bombs ..

devastating aircraft carriers.

can we ever slow the tide,

as we into the valley of

oblivion we ride.

where are the swords you sing of

around your campfires,

knights rescuing damsels

from towers.

rows of bodiacian honest rage.

wild horses,

the fearsome

death spinning wheels

of blade.

Evolved...

****

memories,

sometimes come one at a time

,they sometimes envelope you,

when you are least expecting it,

by the dozen,

as if unfrozen

by the warmth of recollection.

smiles,

long buried ,arise..

and surprise you with

their love

once

again.

almost as though

a fireglow

is touching

your face.

. FIREGLOW
Mounchere.
*****

ELRO.

Jesus Dave. ... great seeing you today.!!

we grew up together,

close as brothers.

The everthorpe crew.

some have left us,

but we, my old mate,

we made it!

i never thought that

i would live to see the day

when i see you with a grey beard.

you old beautiful goat.!

The years just melted away,

in a couple of minutes.

and bev sitting on the sofa,

the core of friendship,

brother and sisterhood,

for over 40 years!!

borstals, kids, homes, approved schools,

detention Centers, me old mate.

The minefield.

And we kicked its fuckin arse.

And i'll tell you what an all,

we will do it again.

it's time for the clans to gather,

and sing old songs,

and tell old yarns,

maybe shed a wee tear

for the lads we were,

and the lassies.

i can't remember a time,

when bev wasn't hangin' about,

somewhere. haha

i want to come home now,

i'm weary of this,

i need a cornish pasty,

and a proper bag of fish and chips.

Not that i haven't met some

superb people over here.

but seeing you both today,

nearly brought me to tears.

still crazy after all these years.

love jimmo.

****

I hear the sea...it's calling to me.
mourning me even,
like a mother wolf..howling
for her young
in the still night
of the forest.
this though.....
this penetrating whisper,
this song of the ancients
beating the shore...
evermore
a lullabye
for the world
and its rage.
her age never destroying
her ways
to beguile.
from her blue gentle loving,
to her flashing
wild eyes.
such thoughts are captured there!!
ocean, ocean, wild gypsy dancer!
and then again,
a slow , seething seducer..
a giver a taker....
an actress a faker,
mischievous , mysterious.
and i am her child.
ALL ABOUT A SEA.
Mounchere.
****

lull me, whilst i follow the flight

of thine angels,

as they skim

across

thy cresting tide,

testing freedoms

of loving winds,

screeching echoes

cross iron skies.

before me lies a rocky shore,

a boat painted red

old rope and barnacles,

timber, sunwashed

and salted.

just ribs now,

like an old sea dog's bones.

bleached and silent,

on the gleaming

green stones.

here the sea hushshshshes

tween seaweed

and shell,

and brings bright coloured pebbles,

in its troughs,

and its swells.

sing me a song from

the sweet pools of time,

send galleons laden

with peace through my mind,

lover of the lonely

and mother

of mankind.

Try to kiss the sky. Try to hold the wind in your arms. Try
to swim in a drop of rain. It would be insane. When love has
gone, packed its bags and rode out of town, all you can do is
save the good times and learn from the rest. Don't get
obsessed, obsession is a prison, an emotionally barred
window that keeps your acceptance in chains and your fear
well fed. You cry only for yourself, perhaps envy sharpens
its poison claws on your sorrow. Tomorrow will come, and
you will welcome it in pain, in a blue mist you have come to
love, need and abhor all the same. I wish you success in your
search for peace. If you do not look for it you will not find
it... And bitterness will shrink your heart, and your soul will
become ill. True love can only live in an open hand, it needs
the space to fly, aye and also the right. I kiss your pain, with
the lips of hope..

****

Heads like a ploughed field,

tumbling thoughts

of

balmy sea´s.

and

drifting sands,

cliffs like some huge

massive giant,

had taken a huge massive bite

from the land.

chalk white.

they stand,..

brooding,waiting, watching.

smugglers caves,

in Robin Hoods Bay.

cobbled ways..leading

from out of the sea.

through the quiet dusk,

and over the moors.

and far away.

There is a pub there

one of the rooms jutts,

out over the cliff.

and the windows catch the spume,

nice place to watch a storm.

This is the place where the

moors meet the ocean.

ages of heather,

lonely skies,

curlews cries,

heavens full on clear nights,

fly to forever.

in winter......

the moors are white,

ghostly silent.

azure blue and indigo sunrise,

from sea to moor,

some thoughts on a sunday afternoon.

Mounchere.

****

THE BLUE ENAMEL TEAPOT.

I was just thinking,

i've held on to this teapot,

longer than any woman

i've ever had in my whole life.

strange that really,

cos they usually take everything.

(in my humble experience of coarse)

though once admittedly,

i was given a lovely yellow plastic sheet

to cover my rucksack with.

because it was raining.

The very majesty of thoughtfulness.

The blue enamel teapot came with me,

many times,

and is still here.

somewhere, somehow, something

is out of whack here.

either i am not normal,

or a complete dick.

take your pick. (but do me a favour and keep it to yourself
eh?)

so yes this blue teapot....

it gurgles wonderful tunes in the mornings,

none of your good morning darlings,

for me mate,

just a soft gurgle, into a red mug.

from an old spout.

Its been repaired twice.

like glued together.Once

after being dropped after me becoming ecstatic

over a piece of burnt toast.

The second time being when i threw

the lid into the

kitchen sink,

and broke that bobbly bit

on the lid.

such larks!!

you can still see the super glue marks.

i wonder if you can be arrested

for teapot abuse.

funny how many thoughts you can get

out of an old teapot,

and it always seems to be around

for the new ones,

we´ve had a few pints together

over the years.

clogged up manys a drainage pipe

with tea leaves.

celebrated the births

of new poems together.

tea rings on the paper.

never tepid,
always the right temperature.

children dying of thirst and hunger
in the desert.
politicians eating supper,
in places of power,
belching and laughing,
as they sit and devour,
all that is put
before them.
pigs at the trough of gold,
just as George Orwell told.
and empathy lies shivering
in the cold.
How can you not give a child
water for its thirst
when you have the choice?
how long could you ignore
a parents pleading voice?
life is not a toy
for you to play with,
you have no right to prescribe death
to innocent fellow humans.
it is your job to execute the promotion
of empathy and freedom,
instead you wallow in your role
of emperor,
you see in a distorted mirror,
narcist, Fascist ,
fool.
your towers will never reach heaven,
and time will steal your jewels.
******

There's a rose erupting from underneath the annual abundance of weeds in the garden.

We'll, it would hardly be in the living room would it?

It comes every year, It's just one thick thorny stalk, with roses on it. The most we've seen here is four. Last year we saw only three, and no.. I don't go hunting flowers to write poetry about,

It's just something to look at from time to time, while I'm drinking my tea. I And they smell of summer. A fine combination indeed, indeed.

Excuse me whilst I get poetic. Let's start with the tea, o majesty of morning brew. Glint of eye, company whilst yawning into existence only to spy the rose.

*****

when all these years,

and all this time,

can just change into a warm light,

years later,

when you are waiting at a bus stop,

one cold winter's night.

****

Under the microscope,

don´t shake my hand then,

i won't die.

i've gotten used to your petty excuses,

and your special brand of snobbery.

look in the mirror man..

tell me what do you see?

two eyes ,a nose, and a mouth

just like me.

*****

once upon a time, a long ,long time ago,

sailed a blue and green orb,

in a space so vast,

its solution,only pure madness

could reflect,

an orb of mists and primal roars,

an orb of silence as deafening as waterfalls.

a place of peace, of colour and wonder,

cracklings of lightings and world ending thunders.

nature gave, and took away,

in perfect harmony,

for itself, and of itself,

for all,and for nothing.

just for the right to sail,

in a space so vast,

only pure madness could

reflect.

****

wolf..sitting on a hill,

on the edge of a wood.

He´s not a young wolf anymore,

his muzzle is grey,

his amber eyes reflect the moon.

soon he mast leave this place,

the world is closing in around him,

he thought the days

of the lone wolf where over,

now he knows they have only just begun.

He has many miles

and many moons to cover,

one last journey into the unknown,

he asks the moon to lend him courage,

he begs his wolfheart to lend him strength,

Head on his paws ,he softly whines for his youth.

His soul licks the dreams he has fulfilled,

and hugs the ones yet to be born.

the children of tomorrow's dawn.

That will grow in quietude,

in solitude and in peace,

far, far away from the petty
squabbles of man.

He stands and shakes himself,
casts his amber over
the twinkling lights below,
and without sorrow,
turns his back and lopes
into the trees,
somehow feeling free,
heads towards unchartered tomorrows.

knowing that the universe
loves a dreamer,
he invites the stars
to light his way.
*****

walking on the shore,

just as the dawn begins to break,

oh how many times before, has

my soul bare and naked,

listened to the songs of the waters

calming melodies.

Aloft the seabirds wheel and glide,

covered now in orange glow,

over bright green rocks fluorescent

in the first kiss of dawn,

greeting the sun with piercing cries

exact wingtips scrape the air.

****

I think i saw your shadow

on the buttercups,

but couldn´t be really sure,

i looked again and it was gone,

only the gold

from the buttercups shone.

strange i don't know your face,

but perhaps had a fleeting glimpse

of your shadow,

amongst some buttercups

in a meadow.

I´ve read your words in colours

i´ve felt the sadness and the joy

i've even shared one of your green frog days,

through the old eyes

of a little boy.

some inspiration is warmly received,

from perhaps a shadow,

in a buttercup field.

******

I wrote a song while you were sleeping,

in those lonely hours just before dawn,

sitting here by my window,

just watching the rain come pouring down,

i hear water gurgling in the gutter,

making its own sweet melody,

now and then booms the thunder,

and i am lost in its symphony.

I wrote these words whilst you were dreaming,

somewhere far away, beside the sea,

somewhere where wild waves are rolling,

far, far, away from me..

trying to find a rhythm in the weather,

something to come together with the rain,

maybe the sound of wind through tree tops?

oh i wish it was a hurricane.

i wrote these words whilst the rain was beating,

tattoos on my window panes,

watching silver streaming by,

in its watery dreamy lanes.

****

Thinking of you today.

Thanks for being there.

These last few months have been dark.

then you came along

with your spark..

words and wisdom,

the fires burning warmly now,

tho frost is at the door,

myself is immersed

in a bath full of peace,

that you with your magic restored.

see you soon,

behind the moon. xx

****

naked she stands now,

her fine gown,

chased up the road

by the wind,

graciously deliciously

swaying in time,

thinly bedecked in

a breath of frost

she was

and she whispered

to me

sweet rhyme.

****

A cut glass of mulled wine
cozy up by the fire,
reflecting flame,
and that beautiful mixture
of contentment...and desire
words become birds
coaxed from the air,
and silence becomes a conversation
with no language nor word.
moving shadows on the ceiling,
fire-glow spilling down the walls,
there is nothing....just this evening,
listen to the silence call.

"Me orchid or orchiding…"

"My daughter says that I look like a 60 year old teenager..hahaha compliments abound!! im 63 next year.hahaha..rock while ya got it man!! hahaha"

winding paths i wandered long,

lonely roads that that love the beat,

of boots upon its grumbling stone,

under trees that whisper secrets

in tongues i do not know,

and silence bids me to listen

until i understand somehow.

sit i sometimes by a shady brook,

and harken the poetry of waters voice,

its liquid lines, with its rushing breath,

gifts me with is a pleasant joy.

...and one time i had such the luck,

to watch a vixen come to drink,

she knew i was there

,always ready for flight,

the flash of amber deft and quick.

i've seen deer standing dreaming

one with with branch and living bough

not one flicker of a movement,

standing though growing from the ground.

eyes dark, but soft as a summer evening,

flash,caught in the noonday sun.

a haughty royal of the forest,

overlooking its kingdom.

many songs of different birds,

tweet, chirp and caw, in lush green crowns,

a buzzard expertly glides the therms,

silent as the snowy clouds.

warmth of summer warms my bones,

as i am near sleep,as insects drone.

an odd airplane splits the sky,

scratches the blue.....and then gone.

you just can´t be in a bad mood here.

the forest laughs at such a thing,

,a mother a father a teacher poet,

listen deeply, can you hear the bluebells ring?

i am home here, not in dear old moltke street.

i turn it all off when i sit in the shade

a different world, full of noisy silence.

a world full of peace,...no plastic facade.

A WEE BIT O WOODS JOY

Mounchere. ..

www.ingramcontent.com/pod-product-compliance
Lightning Source LLC
Chambersburg PA
CBHW051148130726
47988CB00005B/2046